Our Dog T-Bone

A Heartwarming Story of Life with
"One Really Nervous Dog"

by Dan Vander Ark

T-Bone

A Heatwarming Story of Life with One Really Nervous Dog

Our Dog T-Bone
A Heartwarming Story of Life with "One Really Nervous Dog"

by Dan Vander Ark

A.C.V.P.

T-Bone

Our Dog T-Bone
Copyright© 2007 Dan Vander Ark

No part of this book may be copied in any form without
written permission from the copyright owner.

ISBN: 1-934327-16-6

EAN: 978-1-934327-16-6

Cover Design:
3 Five Designs
Duluth, MN 55806

Editor:

Published by
A.C.V.P.
2031 W. Superior St.
Duluth, MN 55806

A Heatwarming Story of Life with One Really Nervous Dog

Table of Contents:

Acknowledgments
Forward
Introduction
A Word About Separation Anxiety
Free Dog 4 Sale: $1,000.00
Rescue the Wedding Shoes
Alcatraz
I'm Gonna See a Shrink!
AARP
The Decision
Running With The Twins
The Face of the Master
We Miss You 'Bone

Acknowledgments

In venturing to write this little book there are several individuals that I need to thank. My parents, Van and Dorothy Vander Ark (my dad passed away in 2002): they instilled in all four of us kids a love for dogs by their own love, appreciation, and patience for the pets they had throughout the years. We each now have our own homes and dogs are a big part of those families. My brother Jan and his wife Ramona had Ghost and now have Oscar, my brother Kevin and his wife Jodie have Maggie, and my sister Lisa and her friend Lori had Alfie and now have Xander.

I also want to thank several of my co-workers – Sandy, Vicki, Nancy, Allen, and Marty. They always listened patiently to the story of T-Bone over the years. Your compassion meant a lot.

I appreciate very much the congregation of Hawthorne (Wisconsin) Assembly of God Church for letting me use the escapades of T-Bone in numerous sermon illustrations. They both laughed and cried as I shared our struggles with his separation anxiety.

A Heatwarming Story of Life with One Really Nervous Dog

Our daughters need to be thanked for their love for T-Bone through his long ordeal – Courtney for first suggesting we get a dog and both Amber and Courtney for being so patient with him. I cannot remember all of the stuff of theirs that he chewed up over the years, but they still loved him unconditionally.

But above all, I want to thank my wife Kay. I can't think of any other way to put it than to simply say that she LOVED "Bone." She didn't grow up with dogs (in fact she had quite a fear of dogs as a child) but she was more than willing to bring him into our home and she grew to love him immensely. My wife will always miss him.

> "To his dog, every man is Napoleon; hence the constant popularity of dogs."
> -- Aldous Huxley

Forward

I only had the privilege of meeting T-bone a few times over his long life, but I feel like I knew him personally through the shared photographs and stories that Dan would bring to work nearly every day. I remember how excited he was when they first got T-bone, the photos of the adorable puppy who was taking over their hearts... and then the long, long struggle to find some way to ease T-bone's anxiety as they went through furniture, appliances, rugs, beds, clothes, shoes and increasingly stronger gates to the laundry room. The patience and compassion the family showed throughout T-bone's ordeals, the choice to hold onto the creature they loved rather than take the easy way out, certainly exemplifies unconditional love in its purest form.

Vicki Strauser

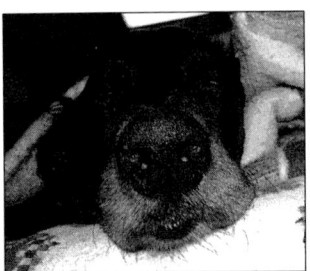

A Heatwarming Story of Life with One Really Nervous Dog

The story of T-Bone is a saga of love and patience that will touch every reader. Having had the pleasure of meeting T-Bone on various occasions over the years, the reading of his story brings laughter and tears. T-Bone's story becomes more than just a heart-wrenching tale of a family's struggle when Dan uses the example of his beloved T-Bone to illustrate God's unconditional love to all of us.

Sandy Scott

"Outside of a dog, a book is man's best friend. Inside of a dog, it's too dark to read."
-- Groucho Marx

The oldest living dog in
the world is either
27 (one claim)
or 29 (another claim)
That's either 189 or 203 people years!

A Heatwarming Story of Life with One Really Nervous Dog

Introduction

"We can judge the heart of a man by
his treatment of animals."
-- Immanuel Kant

"Money will buy you a pretty good dog, but it
won't buy the wag of his tail."
-- Anonymous

Dog -- [dawg, dog] –noun

A domesticated creature and relative of the wolf, bred in about 200 varieties, ranging in size from 4" to 7'. They are carnivores of the family Canidae, they have (unless they have chewed on rocks) prominent canine teeth and a long and slender snout, a muscular body, a bushy tail, and big ears. And they can make the most wonderful faces.

Canis Familiaris T-Bonius

Latin for "four legged furry thing that will steal your heart, chew your stuff, drain you of tears, and seek your face with all of his strength."

A Heatwarming Story of Life with One Really Nervous Dog

Our hearts were broken. Facing a losing battle with separation anxiety and the severity of his old age issues, we knew the time had come. I had called the vet a few days earlier and made an appointment to have T-Bone put to sleep, and now Kay and I and "Bone" made the agonizing trip to the vet clinic. After a few minutes in the waiting area we were ushered into the exam room. I was both crying and shaking, and you could see the tears streaming down my wife's face. When the vet came in he briefly explained to us what he was going to do. Even though T-Bone was mostly blind we both wanted to be in a position to look into his eyes as he passed away. But (as had always been the case at the vet) he was so anxious and struggling so much that I had to sit on the floor and hold him as tight as I could with him straddling my lap. His head was toward my left and I felt bad that I wouldn't be able to look into his eyes but at least I was able to hug him as close as possible. We had tried to prepare ourselves for T-Bone's death, but neither of us was prepared for what he did in the last few moments of his life…..

This is the story of our dog T-Bone. It's the story of a dog but it's also the story of patience, love, and our struggle to cure him of his separation anxiety (S.A.). Along the way we learned some things about life, God's love and patience for people and a cure for the separation anxiety that afflicts us all.

We pray that this story will be a blessing to you all.

Dan & Kay Vander Ark

If you would like to contact Dan or Kay you can email them at: danno.diakonos.duluth@juno.com

A Heatwarming Story of Life with One Really Nervous Dog

A Word about S.A.

"Every boy should have two things: a dog, and a mother willing to let him have one."
-- Anonymous

"To err is human, to forgive canine."
-- Anonymous

The Basenji is the only barkless dog in the world. The oldest breed of dog native to North America is the Chihuahua.

A Heatwarming Story of Life with One Really Nervous Dog

Separation anxiety in dogs (the anxiety of not having their owner within sight), can provoke irrational fears of abandonment. The actual cause of separation anxiety is not easily determined. Among many reasons that canine behavioral specialists give is that it's a predisposition to this type of behavior. But they simply aren't sure. Nevertheless it's a significant problem **which can cause terrific emotional distress for both dogs and their owners.** S.A. can occur at any age in any breed, and is one of the chief reasons for pet owners to put their dogs to sleep or give them away.

Having grown up with dogs (mostly Labs) I knew how a healthy dog should act and what a healthy dog should look like. As this story will relate, from day one T-Bone seemed to be different. Over the years we tried cure after cure, remedy after remedy to try to heal or lessen his anxiety attacks. And when we tell this story to friends and family, a lot of them are amazed that we were so patient with him for so long (perhaps many dogs with his sickness would have gone to that "great dog-house in the sky" at a much earlier age). But we were always willing to try one more thing or give him one more chance -- and at times it seemed that he was getting better. But then something (that we could never put our finger on) would trigger his anxiety and it seemed that we would go back to square one. As I look back I realize that perhaps there are some things we should have done differently with T-Bone and I am sure that we made some training mistakes with him along the way (parents sometimes say the same thing when they look back at how they raised their kids). But as the story will relate, throughout T-Bone's life we sought wisdom from family, friends and professionals in a hope of lessening or curing his separation anxiety disorder so that he might live a good dog-life. So one of our hopes is that, after reading this story, if you are struggling with a pet that suffers from separation anxiety, you will be willing to exercise the utmost patience and love for your dog.

A Heatwarming Story of Life with One Really Nervous Dog

Free Dog For Sale: $1,000.00

"A dog teaches a boy fidelity, perseverance, and to turn around three times before lying down."
-- Robert Benchley

"You can say any foolish thing to a dog, and the dog will give you a look that says, "My God, you're right! I never would've thought of that!"
-- Dave Barry

Apparently the haircut of the Poodle was originally meant to improve their swimming abilities as a retriever. And the pom-poms were left in place to warm their joints.

Fifi...go get that duck. And don't get your pom-poms wet!!!

A Heatwarming Story of Life with One Really Nervous Dog

One day T-Bone and I were sitting together eating Oreos and just enjoying the day (I "unscrewed" the cookies and somehow he always chose the part with the creamy frosting...go figure). Anyway, I asked him, "You know the only difference between you and me? No, beside the fact that you have hair and I don't." He didn't know so I told him, "My Thumb!" I went on to explain, "Just think what you could do if you had a thumb. You could master the doorknob principle, you could escape from prison and lie on the futon and yes, you could even use the TV remote!" Dan & T-Bone

In 1992 our youngest daughter Courtney, who was 12 at the time, began asking if we could get a dog. I was raised in a family that always had dogs so my heart immediately wanted to say YES! But with both my wife and I working full-time and the kids in school we knew it wouldn't work out at that time. But when Christmas came I had an idea. I made a "Free Dog Coupon" out of a picture of some cute Labrador puppies and then wrote a letter to my daughter, "Courtney, you can redeem this coupon for one dog of your choice when school is out in June. This is my promise to you…Merry Christmas!" I put the letter and the coupon in a manila envelope and hid it beside the chair I was sitting in when we opened our Christmas gifts. All the gifts were opened and then I handed her the unmarked envelope. As she read it tears came to her eyes, tears came to her sister's eyes, tears came to my eyes, and fire came out of my wife's eyes. Just kidding…fire did not come out of her eyes…just laser beams (actually, she loved T-Bone as much as any of us and deserves a medal for her extraordinary patience with the "Bone" over the years).

> HAPPY, adorable Lab mix puppies, Free to country homes. 728-

Well, late spring rolled around and we began searching the classifieds for a "Free Dog" (just a little side issue here...with all the laws that Congress enacts it seems to me that they would have made a decree to put an asterisk and disclaimer by any classified ads for pets that contains the word "FREE"; the disclaimer would simply have to say, "Please note the above aforementioned FREE dog will actually cost you several thousand dollars"). We eventually found an ad for free lab pups and took the plunge to go check out the puppies. There were a handful of 8 week old lab/setter mix puppies that had already attended the "pick-me-oh-pleeeeaaase-pick-me-I'm-the-cutest" school of deception. We picked up several of them and finally decided on a male that seemed to be pretty mellow (he actually came over and laid his head down on my wife's shoe! Must have been an "A" student). We found out he was born on April 15th -- tax day. So I wanted to name him "1040" or "Short Form" but I didn't think that would sound to good if I had to shout out the back door, "1040, where are you? Come on boy!" He got his name "T-Bone" from a pet on one of the kids' TV shows. My former boss one time asked me, "How's Porkchop?" I said, "His name is T-Bone." "Oh," she said, "I knew he was in the meat group."

That summer we trained him some and he trained us some. He was housebroken in just a couple of days and so we concluded, "This dog-owning thing ain't gonna be so bad." But a hint of what we were in for over the next 13

A Heatwarming Story of Life with One Really Nervous Dog

years came a couple of days after the kids went back to school in the fall. On Labor Day weekend we tested him out by leaving him alone for a good part of the day and he seemed to be fine. "Seemed" is the key word here. A couple of days into the school year I came home from work (the kids got home about 3:30 and I got home about 4:30) and I heard the vacuum cleaner running as I came up to the front door of our double-wide mobile home. "Well that's nice, the kids are cleaning the house," I thought. But a scene of horror and devastation was waiting just behind the door. When I opened the door Courtney was trying to vacuum up dirt.... and lots of dirt. Kay had (past tense) an abundance of beautiful house plants arrayed by the front picture window...but they were now bits of destroyed greenery immersed in lots and lots of dirt. The vacuum was stuffed so full that the suction was almost non-existent and the dirt just rolled out the end of the hose. My wife had also just watered all the plants that morning so it was muddy dirt, and muddy dirt tracked throughout the house. Courtney and Amber must have thought when they opened the door, that that was going to be the end of T-Bone. And as they cleaned they were probably thinking about funeral arrangements. "But hey, he's a pup," we thought, "he'll grow out of it." We thought wrong.

> "Things that upset a terrier may pass virtually unnoticed by a Great Dane."
> -- Smiley Blanton

A Heatwarming Story of Life with One Really Nervous Dog

Rescue The Wedding Shoes

"No animal should ever jump up on the dining-room furniture unless absolutely certain that he can hold his own in the conversation."
-- Fran Lebowitz

"We've begun to long for the pitter-patter of little feet – so we bought a dog. Well, it's cheaper, and you get more feet."
-- Rita Rudner

T-Bone

There are 42 teeth in a dog's mouth.
In Paulding, Ohio, a policeperson is allowed to
bite a dog in order to quiet him

A Heatwarming Story of Life with One Really Nervous Dog

> It was the day after Thanksgiving and T-Bone and I shared a piece of pumpkin pie. "Man T-Bone!" I recoiled, "You have the breath of a thousand dead Pharaohs! It's no wonder you have a hard time finding a girlfriend..."
>
> Dan & T-Bone

We figured out what to do with "Bone" when we were at work and the kids were at school so that there would be no more plant destruction (we had tried to kennel him when he was real young but it came to the point where he was either going to destroy the kennel or himself). In the fall of 1994 we moved into a house just a couple of blocks from where the kids went to school and things went so-so with T-Bone for quite a while. For a while he was able to roam about the house when we were gone and when the kids were at school – at least some of the time it seemed he lounged out on the three season porch and kept watch out the windows, waiting for school to let out. The kids left for school around 8:00, he was alone until they came home for lunch and then again until about 3:30. One time, however, he somehow locked himself in our daughter's bedroom and destroyed her closet door and hamper. There was more than one bedspread and comforter that found his wrath, and because he got up on the couch and clawed at the cushions we had to set a couple of dining room chairs on that piece of furniture each morning before we left for work. (I know, I know....I know exactly what women everywhere who love their living rooms and couches are thinking...would Martha Stewart do that?) But when we got home the chairs and sometimes even the cushions would be knocked onto the floor. And the window sills in the porch showed more than a few teeth marks as a result of his daily vigil of waiting for the kids.

For a time we locked him in the basement but he seemed to be able to bang on the door long enough to jimmy it open. We eventually had to replace that door because it was in such terrible shape (have you ever seen "Turner and Hooch"? It wasn't quite that bad, but close).

Let me pause for a moment because many reading this may be wondering to themselves, "WHY ON EARTH DID YOU KEEP THE DOG???" (As I write this and think back over these events I sometimes wonder the same thing). The bottom line is...we loved him! And I guess it seemed that we were always willing to try one more solution, we were always willing to buy one more couch (not really). He would seem to get better, then digress, get better, and then get worse again.

A turning point came on a muggy Friday night in July, 1999 during our oldest daughter's wedding rehearsal. We were gone for a few hours and hadn't realized that some severe thunderstorms rolled through the area while we were in the church. We came home to a disaster. Many dogs get hyper and nervous during thunderstorms but for T-Bone those weather events just seemed to magnify his multiple anxieties (we got some of those "thunderstorm pills" for him at one point. The prescription label clearly read, "Give One Pill One Hour Before Thunderstorm." Huh? Do they come with a barometer and a weather man?)

A couple of doors in our newly remodeled basement were scratched but when we went upstairs to our bedroom it truly looked as if an F3 tornado had gone through that area. It was a disaster. The furniture wasn't destroyed but it seemed that just about everything else was. Chewed up "Martha Stewart" magazines littered the floor, the contents of my wife's sewing box was everywhere (how he managed not to swallow some pins and needles I will never know). He had gotten into the closet and wreaked havoc. But worst of all it looked like he had destroyed my wife's brand new light green wedding day shoes (the ones that perfectly matched the mother-of-the-bride dress). The box was totally annihilated and shredded – it apparently fought valiantly against the "beast" and gave its life so that the shoes could escape. Because there, in the midst of the rubble, lay the shoes without a mark or scratch on them! Good thing for the dog – chewing up a truck seat is one thing (more on this later), but chewing up wedding day shoes brings a dog very very close to doggie heaven. My theory is that God sent a couple of rookie angels (perhaps Angels-In-Training) to rescue "the shoes":

<u>*God:*</u> Your mission is to go to the Milky Way Galaxy, the Solar System, Planet Earth, the North American Continent, the United States, and the

state of Minnesota. There in a northern city is a crazed dog that is about to go totally berserk. Your mission, should you choose to accept it, is to SAVE THE WEDDING SHOES! Now Go, Go, Go with the Goodness of Cheerios!

Angel in Training One: Come on, we're never gonna get there in time!!! "Now Dasher! Now Dancer! Now, Prancer and Vixen! On, Comet! On, Cupid! On, Donner and Blitzen! To the top of the porch! To the top of the wall! Now dash away! Dash away! Dash away all!"

Angel in Training Two (with a totally baffled look on his face): Like uh dude, ain't you in the wrong story?

Angel in Training Two (somewhere far above planet Earth): Hurry – he's almost done chewing up the last Martha Stewart magazine.

Angel in Training One (mystically blasting his way through the walls of our house): He's got the box! Stop Him! He's got The Box!!!!

__T-Bone__: What was THAT? I'm nervous enough and now some feathered arm just grabbed those shoes out of my mouth. Valium, valium, valium, I NEED Valium!

__Angel in Training One__: The box, he's chewing up the box! Can he have the box? Check the orders!

__Angel in Training Two__: Uhmmmm, let's see, rule 6, chapter 3, subparagraph 2: "said crazy dog T-Bone with multiple anxieties is allowed to destroy the box." HE CAN HAVE THE BOX!!!

He was panting so feverishly that it took several hours for him to completely calm down. We cleaned up the room and the other parts of the house and tried to make things presentable for people coming over the next couple of days. We were truly at a loss as to what to do with him, but in a few days we thought we had come up with another solution. Again though, we thought wrong.

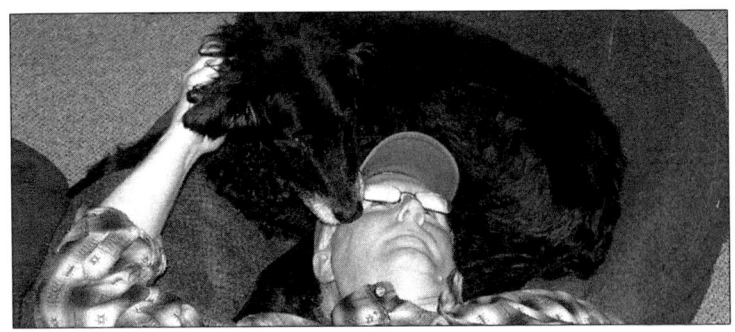

6/100ths of a second! That's all it takes for dogs to locate the source of a sound. They can apparently swivel their ears like radar dishes. I'll bet it takes longer for husband dogs…

A Heatwarming Story of Life with One Really Nervous Dog

Alcatraz

"I wonder if other dogs think poodles are members of a weird religious cult."
-- Rita Rudner

"The average dog is a nicer person than the average person."
-- Andy Rooney

"Did you ever walk into a room and forget why you walked in? I think that's how dogs spend their lives."
-- Sue Murphy

The laundry room in the basement of our house is built like a bomb shelter: concrete block walls all the way around with one little window at about the 6' level. It's a 6' x 15' foot room with a freezer on one end, shelves along one wall, and a washer and dryer on the other end. Perfect! The floor had glued-down indoor-outdoor carpeting, the washer/dryer/freezer are made out of high quality steel and I put doors over the shelves up to 4' high so he couldn't get to anything he shouldn't get into. I made a plywood 4'x4' "door" for the opening to the laundry room and covered it with some pretty tough carpeting (there was a hollow-core mahogany door on there but I knew that it would be toast in no time at all). I made a couple of latches to fasten it to the opening and thought, "This should hold him."

It didn't. We came home and he was out...he didn't go over the makeshift door, he somehow broke the latches and hinges and sort of went through it! And the carpeting that covered it was shredded. I thought, "Well I just didn't latch it good enough." I remade and recovered the door and reinforced the latches. I have a four year college degree – I'm smarter than the dog. This should hold him!

It didn't. We came home and he was out...but this time stuff inside the laundry room was destroyed. A lot of the glued down carpeting was pulled up. But most bizarrely – the washer and dryer were moved out of their places! The washer was moved (if you have ever had to move one of those you know how heavy they are) and the dryer was pushed out as far as the cord would allow. The dryer vent duct was ripped off and smashed. We were dumbfounded.

It took a long time, but we cleaned it up, ripped up the remaining carpeting, and painted the floor. I put blocks in between the washer and dryer and the walls so they couldn't be moved.

I want to pause again just to mention a couple things. Through this long, stressful ordeal we had talked to friends who were dog owners, researched separation anxiety on the internet and other places, and talked with our vet – all in desperate attempts to try to figure out what to do with T-Bone. We made sure he had plenty of exercise – I consistently took him jogging and my wife faithfully walked him a couple of miles every day. But many, many times we were in tears trying to decide if we should put him to sleep and more than once I talked with my parents about what to do with him. At one point my dad strongly suggested that we put him down, and, as any dog-lover would, we struggled and agonized with that option. We talked about giving him away, but we honestly wondered about who would be willing to put up with him. And as you read this, all of these events may seem sort of "time-compressed," but there were seasons and periods of time (as I mentioned earlier) that he honestly seemed to be getting better. The house would be in good order or the blankets in his room would hardly be out of place. But then for some inexplicable reason he would slip back into his severe separation anxiety mode.

Back to Alcatraz. I found that a chain link kennel door from our local home improvement store fit perfectly inside the door opening of the laundry room. I thought I had come up with the perfect solution. No way for him to bang/chew/dig/blast his way through that. The hinges were bolted directly into the concrete. It was Saturday when I

A Heatwarming Story of Life with One Really Nervous Dog

finished. We put him in there on Sunday about 8:30 AM and then headed off to church. When we got home about 1:00 I walked up to the front door and could hear him barking. But I immediately thought to myself, "His barking is a lot louder than it should be if he was still in the laundry room!" When I opened the front door I could not believe my eyes! My mouth just dropped open as I wondered out loud, "HOW DID YOU GET OUT OF THERE?!"

I literally ran down the stairs to figure out his method of escape. He had somehow wedged himself between the tubular frame of the kennel door and the chain link mesh. But to do that he had to first bend two heavy duty "clips" that held the chain link to the frame. I have taken a pair of vise grip pliers and tried bending one of those clips myself and have a hard time doing it. I gave one of them to someone I was telling this story to (he was about six foot something and weighed about 225 lbs.) – he couldn't bend it! I said, "You know, my dog only weighs 75lbs…"

On Monday (I took the day off from work because of "dog") I went back to the home improvement store. I put two layers of chain link on the door and reinforced it with steel and put a sign on it: "ALCATRAZ." He never escaped from there although occasionally I took down his Lassie and Scooby-Doo posters just to make sure he wasn't digging through the walls like some sort of canine Tim Robbins in "The Shawshank Redemption."

> "Don't accept your dog's admiration as conclusive evidence that you are wonderful."
>
> -- Ann Landers

A Heatwarming Story of Life with One Really Nervous Dog

I'm Gonna See A Shrink!

"Dogs feel very strongly that they should always go with you in the car, in case the need should arise for them to bark violently at nothing right in your ear."
-- Dave Barry

T-Bone and I were going for a ride in my old Nissan truck. I looked over at him, he was leaning back on the seat, looking so contented with his tongue just barely hanging out. I'm almost positive I heard him ask, "Is this heaven?" "No," I said, "This is my truck." He looked out the windshield and replied, "Oh, I could've sworn this was heaven."
-- Dan & T-Bone

A 3-year-old Great Dane in
California, is apparently
the world's tallest dog –
he is 7 feet tall when upright.
Watch out Shaq…

A Heatwarming Story of Life with One Really Nervous Dog

After some time he seemed to settle down yet again, and for a lengthy period of time we would come home and find that his blankets had hardly been moved. (The question my wife and I would always ask of the one who got home from work first was, "How was his room?") But as always, something would "trigger" inside of his dog mind and he would again go through a season of panic and anxiety attacks. Once we came home and he had somehow gotten through the end of the shelving unit in the laundry room (where we never even imagined he could get into) and had chomped through a couple of plastic and steel paint cans. Fortunately when he was all done destroying the paint cans they landed with the puncture wounds "up" so that all of the paint didn't run out. Good thing he didn't have latex allergies.

We would put him in his room but he still wasn't happy -- something else had to be done with him. I made an appointment with the local vet and brought some pictures to show him. He was a "veteran" veterinarian and had been around a long time and seen a lot of dog "stuff." But you could tell he was surprised by what T-Bone was going through. I asked him for his advice. Two things still stand out clearly from that conversation. He told me the story of a guy who also struggled with a dog suffering from separation anxiety. His solution? He took a mannequin and dressed the dummy in some of his clothes. Over time he gradually kept removing a piece of the mannequin. I can't remember the total length of time it took but at one point he removed a leg, then an arm, then another leg, than another arm, then the head (not sure if that's the correct magical sequence)….so eventually it was just the torso clothed with one of his t-shirts. Finally, the torso was removed and just the t-shirt was left. Apparently the dog bought it – eventually all he had to do was leave an unwashed T-shirt and the dog thought the master was still home. I wonder if the dog ever thought while all of that was going on, "I wonder why my master is being so lazy today, doesn't he have to go to work? And I swear he seems to be getting smaller. But it sure smells like him so I guess he must be here."

The other item that stood out from the conversation? "Your dog may need to see a shrink!" It wasn't phrased exactly like that but that was the thrust of it. Now I was the person who made fun of people who dressed their dogs in little coats and who took their dogs to doggie psychiatrists, but we were at the end of our rope. So we asked him to make an appointment with an "animal behavior specialist" at the University of Minnesota Vet Clinic.

We drove the 150 miles to the clinic and were ushered into a little exam room. I half-way expected to see a small leather couch for him to lie down on. I imagined that maybe the exam would go like this….

Behavior Specialist (in her best Dr. Freud voice): Zo, T-Bone, pleaze lie down on ze couch and tell me about yourselv and your problemz…

T-Bone (in his best doggie patient voice): Well Doc, I just get so nervous and I don't understand myself. I don't mean to chew up all that stuff (although my master said that when I chewed up all those Martha Stewart magazines that that was ok), and I feel so bad after I do it that I just hate myself. I know my master loves me and I am sooooooooooooooooooo glad that he and his wife are so patient with me. I over-heard them talking about me one time (they didn't know I was nearby) that they might have to put me to sleep. Now Doc I don't know what that means exactly, I just know they both sounded so very sad when they were talking about it so I knew it couldn't be good. If you could just help me not to be so nervous and get so filled with anxiety...I'm just not happy unless I see my master's face and when I don't, I panic. Please help me doc – I don't know how much longer I can go on like this. I will give you as many doggy biscuits as you want if you can help me.

With me in the room, the doctor and her assistant watched T-Bone for awhile. She immediately recognized the "anxious smile" and witnessed first hand his panting and shaking and constant pacing. Her diagnosis? She gave him a prescription for a sort of "doggie Ritalin" and instructed us on how to try to reprogram/retrain him. "Is there anything that triggers his anxiety and is there some common or consistent thing that you do that lets him know you are leaving for the day?" Well, let's see – what triggers his anxiety? How about the microwave (honestly), the toaster oven, the regular oven, CNN, cooking, baking, people visiting, people not visiting, little kids, thunderstorms, clouds, leaves falling, in other words: EVERYTHING! And is there something consistent we do that lets him know we are leaving for the day? Well, we both take showers, get dressed and have breakfast. We have to altar that routine? Well I ain't giving up eating and I ain't going to work naked, so how about we skip the shower part? "No idiot," she snarled as she glared at me (not really – she was very, very nice and very, very compassionate). "No," she said, "I mean it could be something as simple as the sound of picking up your car keys that triggers his anxiety. Can you alter your routine? Go out a different door, have your clothes packed and go out the door in your pajamas (honestly, she suggested this, I'm not making this up). Somehow you have to alter your routine."

Well we left. I was now suffering from separation anxiety myself (my money had separated from my billfold). We got him the prescription and kept him on it for awhile but took him off from it because he lost his playfulness and seemed to be in a stupor (plus, the behavioral specialist informed us that the medicine was only meant to assist in retraining him and wasn't meant to be a permanent solution). And we did try to alter our routines – I ate my cornflakes in the truck as I was driving to work! Seriously, we did do some things differently but it didn't help. I realize some people would say that we weren't consistent or patient enough in trying to "reprogram" him, or that we should have used more of the "tough-love" approach and that any dog can be trained to handle his persistent anxiety. Maybe so, but after having lived with "Bone" for so many years I doubt it.

Dogs in Pennsylvania seeking to congregate in groups of three or more on private property must first have a permit signed by the mayor.

T-Bone

A woman in Europe is claiming
to be the owner of the
world's smallest dog.
The dog is four inches tall
at the shoulder.
He is four inches from nose to tail
and weighs just over a pound.

A Heatwarming Story of Life with One Really Nervous Dog

AARP

"I've seen a look in dogs' eyes, a quickly
vanishing look of amazed contempt, and I am
convinced that basically
dogs think humans are nuts."
-- John Steinbeck

"In dog years I'm dead"
--Anonymous

"My dog is worried about the economy because Alpo is up to 99 cents a can. That's almost $7.00 in dog money."
-- Joe Weinstein

A Heatwarming Story of Life with One Really Nervous Dog

Over his time in Alcatraz things had their ups and downs. My wife thought it would be a good idea if we went to Goodwill and bought him a nice comfortable, cushiony chair for him to lie down in when we were gone. We went all out and spent $10.00. The chair lost. And only lasted one day. Just the frame was intact. Foam rubber and stuffing and upholstery everywhere. No more chairs.

That reminds me. I almost forgot to tell you about "The Day the Dog Ate the Truck Seat." We were in the midst of building a new church and in the fall of that year on a mid-October drizzly sort of day I took T-Bone with me in my pickup and brought him to the work-site. Many times in the past I had taken him along with me in the truck and he was perfectly fine. But not that Saturday. Around noon it started to rain so I put him in the truck but I checked on him often and let him out frequently to get some exercise. But at about 4:00 I left for the day and opened the truck door only to be greeted by chunks of foam rubber. That's never a good sign. The driver's seat was toast. On the way home I said to him, "I hope you enjoyed the foam rubber because that's all you're getting to eat tonight."

He shredded more blankets than we could count. Even though they looked like Swiss cheese, at times we still took them outside to shake them out. We wondered what the neighbors thought.

But most days during the last couple years of his life we would come home and his room wasn't too bad – the blankets were messed up, but overall things didn't look that bad. And sometimes when I came home, instead of hollering "T-Bone!" right away I would sneak

A Heatwarming Story of Life with One Really Nervous Dog

over to his laundry room/kennel door (he was pretty hard of hearing) to see what he was doing – and guess what? HE WOULD ACTUALLY BE LYING DOWN!

When he was about 12 I took him for a walk through the woods and I forgot to make sure he was right beside me when I made the turn on the trail to go back to the vehicle. I went about a ¼ mile and suddenly realized he was nowhere in sight. I panicked. I ran back up the trail and could see him a long way off silhouetted against the night sky. I yelled as loud as I could but he couldn't hear me and I could tell he was looking for me. I kept running as fast as my out-of-shape body could carry me fearing that he might wander off into the woods. Fortunately he just sort of stayed in one spot looking around until I got there. From that moment on I had to put him on a leash whenever we went walking. In the last year of his life when I took him for a walk he could only go a short distance. He was almost completely blind, he was almost completely deaf, and he limped from arthritis. But still, when you would say, "Get your leash!" his adrenalin kicked in and he would wag his tail and bark excitedly.

Most days when we put him into the laundry room he was fine. And sometimes he would just walk right in and start eating his snacks without a seeming care in the world. One day I was in a hurry to get to work (my wife would say that's my usual mode) and just as I was heading out the door I realized I hadn't put T-Bone in lockdown and shut his door. I turned around and he was standing in the laundry room doorway looking out at me as if to say, "Maybe if I don't move he won't realize he forgot to shut the door. And I can raid the fridge and sit on the futon and watch Animal Planet when he's gone!" I honestly laughed to myself when I saw his expression.

But some days, and for whatever reason, he would just shake when he went into his room. And at times (though not frequently) we would really have to coax him to get him in. And even when we were at home he would sometimes slip into his anxiety mode and we had to holler "T-Bone!" to get him out of that zone. When I had visited my parents on occasion there would be

A Heatwarming Story of Life with One Really Nervous Dog

four dogs (all Labs) that would roam around their lake home property: Maggie, Tomack, Max, and T-Bone. And sometimes Maggie, Tomack and Max would be laying down sleeping but T-Bone would be panting and pacing until it seemed he almost wore himself out, and then he would finally lay down. When T-Bone was about 10, at Christmas time I called the vet and asked him if there was anything he could prescribe for the dog for Christmas Eve. People were coming over and with all the commotion and cooking I knew T-Bone was going to have a

hard time. He gave the dog a prescription for just a few pills of Valium. He took two and I took the rest....just kidding......I took all of them…..no, not really, T-Bone took two and I ate turkey.

When my wife and I look back we are so very glad that we were so patient with him. Sure, we got frustrated and upset with him (and maybe he did with us), but we loved him and were so very glad he was a part of the family. When you're a kid and the family dog dies, their passing can almost rip your heart out. I remember our dog Max getting hit by a car when I was a teenager and still vividly recall the little funeral we had for him in the corner of the lot at our rural home. It isn't easier when you grow up. I talked to my older brother on Christmas day, 2005 – he called to see how our Christmas had gone. We chatted for awhile and as we were saying our good-byes I said, "Well, say hi to Moe and Scott and Ghost." He couldn't say hi to Ghost he said, Ghost had just died. My eyes welled up with tears, and you could hear the emotions in his voice. His dog Ghost (a big, mellow, lovable white shepherd mix) and our dog T-Bone were only a month apart in age. I asked him what happened and he told me what had transpired the last couple of weeks: Ghost had some sort of inflammation in his jaw which swelled up severely so they took him to the vet to check him out, and because he didn't improve they took him to a specialist. But the swelling went down and it seemed he was going to be ok. My brother took him for a short walk but Ghost was so weak he couldn't make it back and died a couple of hours later. It was hard for him to tell the story and we both cried.

The lyrics of "Mr. Bojangles" talk about the deep bond that lives on between a dog and his master when Jerry Jeff Walker wrote "…His dog up and died, he up and died; after twenty years he still grieves…"

Sir Walter Scott said, "I have sometimes thought of the final cause of dogs having such short lives and I am quite satisfied it is in compassion to the human race; for if we suffer so much in losing a dog after an acquaintance of ten to twelve years, what would it be if they were to double?"

"The Dog was created especially for children. He is the god of frolic."
-- Henry Ward Beecher

"Man himself cannot express love and humility by external signs so plainly as does a dog, when with dropping ears, hanging lips…and wagging tail, he meets his beloved master."
-- Charles Darwin

"All knowledge, the totality of all questions and answers, is contained in the dog."
-- Franz Kafka

A Heatwarming Story of Life with One Really Nervous Dog

Blossoms along old highway 61 the day of his last walk

The Decision

"He is your friend, your partner, your defender, your dog. You are his life, his love, his leader. He will be yours, faithful and true, to the last beat of his heart. You owe it to him to be worthy of such devotion."
--Anonymous

"A dog is the only thing on earth that loves you more than he loves himself."
--Josh Billings

If a dog's prayers were answered, bones would rain from the sky."
-- Old Proverb

A Heatwarming Story of Life with One Really Nervous Dog

It was Friday, May 12th. I left for work at 7:30 and came home at about 2:00 to check on Bone. I was amazed...he was sleeping so peacefully (in fact I had to watch him for a few moments to make sure he was still breathing) and his room looked as if I had put him in just a few seconds earlier. His blankets weren't even wrinkled and his dog dish was not moved so much as an inch! Most times I would just sneak back up stairs, grab something to eat and head back to work, but this day I wanted to see him. He heard me rattling the door and he slowly realized that "Hey, the master's home, but it ain't 5:00 yet!" We went upstairs, I grabbed something to eat, he lay down beside me and I read for a few minutes before I headed back to work. I let him out to do his business and then put him back in his room and I went back to work.

I came home at about 4:45 and could not believe my eyes. It was more than just a bout with separation anxiety – it was a site of total chaos and he was in an absolute panic mode. At that moment I knew that he could not go on. Before I even let him out I called the vet and, with a trembling voice, I asked to make an appointment for a few days out to have T-Bone put to sleep.

Kay came home a few minutes later. I broke down when I told her that he could not go on any longer like this and that I had called the vet. She reluctantly agreed and we both cried. I cleaned up his room and gave him a bath.

The next day we informed the kids of our decision. They were well aware of what was going on with him and, even though it was hard, they supported our decision. I wanted to make the appointment a few days out so we could really weigh what we were doing and also have enough time to say goodbye. Suddenly, the past 13 years with Bone seemed to have been far, far too short. Kay and I both made arrangements to take that Thursday off. I emailed my coworkers that I had to be gone that day to tend to a family matter.

> "Qui me amat, amet et canem meum."
> (Who loves me will love my dog also)
> -- St. Bernard

"There is honor in being a dog."
-- Aristotle

A Heatwarming Story of Life with One Really Nervous Dog

Running With The Twins

"Dear Master," I explained to Saint Peter, "I'd rather stay here, outside the Pearly Gates. I won't be a nuisance, I won't even bark, I'll be very patient and wait. I'll be here, chewing on a celestial bone no matter how long you may be. I'd miss you so much if I went in alone. It wouldn't be heaven for me.
-- Unknown

"If I have any beliefs about immortality, it is that certain dogs I have known will go to heaven, and very, very few persons."
--James Thurber

"In the beginning,
God created man,
but seeing him so feeble,
He gave him the dog."
-- Toussenel

A Heatwarming Story of Life with One Really Nervous Dog

That next Thursday we both got up early and I went and sat out on our little back deck. I brought T-Bone's bed out there and as I read my Bible and drank some coffee I couldn't believe that he was actually laying down in it. Normally he would be in his pacing mode, but maybe he just thought, "You know, its nice out, my master's next to me, I'm kind of tired today, I think I'm gonna just lay down for awhile." I would read a little bit, watch him for a little while, and through tears think, "Why couldn't you just be normal?"

About 9:00 he and I hopped in my rusty truck and I took him up by old highway 61 for one last walk on the trail. I opened the truck door but his sight was so bad he didn't even know it was open. In fact he just started walking toward the door like he was walking down the sidewalk not really realizing he was a couple feet off the ground. If I hadn't caught him he would have just tumbled out the door. It was a warm sunshiny day and we slowly walked for about an hour and then came home. Around noon Kay and I took some pictures of him with the both of us and at about 1:00 I got his leash and took him out to the garage. He had never ridden in our new truck before (it wasn't really new I guess, just new to me -- it was actually a 1998 S-10 in immaculate condition). I told T-Bone when I had gotten it several months earlier that he was never gonna ride in the "new" truck, just the one that had the good tasting truck seat. I backed out the S-10 and said, "Hey buddy, want to go for a ride in the new truck?"

The trip to the vet seemed like a blur – we both had to keep wiping the tears from our eyes. My wife asked me several times if I was sure that we should do this and I agonizingly said yes. We pulled into the vet clinic and waited a few minutes in the reception area. Several "normal" dogs were there and again I wished that T-Bone could have been like them. The tech called us into the room and she informed us that the doctor would come in whenever we were ready. After a few minutes we informed her that we were ready and he came in. Anytime T-Bone visited the vet we pretty much had to sit on him or back him into a corner and hold him real tight whenever they drew blood or gave him a shot. On this day the vet wanted to do the injection in the right front leg. We struggled with him for a little and then I just sat on the floor with him straddling my lap with his face toward my left. We both wanted so much to look into his face when he passed on but because of his anxiety I wouldn't be able to. Kay knelt down next to me and next to T-Bone's face -- I held him

tighter than I had ever held him before. I asked the doc how long it would take and he said that he would be gone very quickly once he started the injection. He asked if we were ready. That's a hard question to answer. With a broken heart I said, "Yes."

He started the injection. In the last few seconds of T-Bone's life he did something so remarkable that neither of us will ever forget it – something that will forever be etched in our memories. Whether he knew how bad I wanted to look him in the face, or he just desperately wanted to look into the face of his master one last time, we will never know. But with all the strength that he could muster he craned his neck and bent his head as far back as he possibly could so that I could see his face and look into his eyes. And then he suddenly slumped in my arms and was gone.

For several minutes we both just sat on the floor and cried. I remember repeating over and over again, "I love you T-Bone, I love you T-Bone." Kay gently closed his eyes.

We went out to the truck and cried some more. We didn't really know what to do next...we just knew we didn't want to go home for awhile.

We both realized this day was coming and when we finally had to make the decision to have T-Bone put to sleep we tried to prepare ourselves. But to be honest with you I wasn't prepared for three things. First, how much it hurt that he was gone. I talked to my brother a few days afterward and he said the same thing about the loss of their dog Ghost. For years Ghost had gone with him every morning to go out and get the paper. "You try to continue that same habit," he said, "but then realize your canine friend isn't there anymore." The second thing neither of us was prepared for was how empty the house seemed to be without him. I definitely see why people who love dogs don't wait too long before they get another one. The new dog can't completely fill the void of the previous pet, but they can help. And thirdly, I knew Kay loved T-Bone tremendously, but I honestly didn't realize the depth of her love for Bone. A couple of days after T-Bone passed on we were talking in the kitchen and she started crying. There was such a look of loss on her face – a look that said, "I'd put up with anything from him just to be able to hold him one more time."

Somewhere during those first couple of days after T-Bone was gone, Kay said something that brought a tearful smile to my face. "Boney is running with the twins," she said. I knew immediately what she meant. In May of 2004 our youngest daughter and her husband lost their twins – a boy and a girl. They would do their growing up in heaven. "T-Bone's not nervous anymore, he's over his battle with separation anxiety, he can see, he can hear and he can run with the twins," Kay said through tears. Do dogs (and other pets) go to heaven? Theologians who are a lot smarter than me have argued both ways about what the Bible has to say about the pet-afterlife stuff. But I lean toward the fact that we will see our pets in heaven (and I think that dogs will slide right on in without any hassle; cats on the other hand will need to have a passport, two other forms of picture ID, and must have completed 2000 hours of community service). I guess the bottom line is that I know that I know that I know that we serve a good God and that the blessings of heaven go far beyond our wildest imaginations. I Corinthians 2:9 reminds us, "...no mere man or woman has ever seen, heard, or even imagined what wonderful things God has ready for those who love the Lord." (TLB). So I kind of like to think that Bone is really enjoying himself up there and that Jesus has taken him for a couple of walks (or at least one of His angels has). And I also like to think that everyday he stops by one of the gates of the City, looks out with a longing gaze and wonders if this is the day that his master will show up.

"I have sometimes thought of the final cause of dogs having such short lives and I am quite satisfied it is in compassion to the human race; for if we suffer so much in losing a dog after an acquaintance of ten to twelve years, what would it be if they were to double?"
-- Sir Walter Scott

A Heatwarming Story of Life with One Really Nervous Dog

The Face of the Master

"Heaven goes by favour. If it went by merit, you
would stay out and your dog would go in."
--Mark Twain

"I care not for a man's religion whose dog and cat
are not the better for it."
--Abraham Lincoln

T-Bone

Near this spot are deposited
the remains of one who possessed beauty
without vanity, strength
without insolence, courage
without ferocity,
and all the virtues of man
without his vices.
This praise, which would
be unmeaning flattery if
inscribed over human ashes,
is but a just tribute to the memory of
"Boatswain" a dog, who was born at
Newfoundland, May 1803
and died at Newstead Abbey,
November 18, 1808.
John Cam Hobhouse/Lord Byron

Over the 13+ years with T-Bone he taught us a lot about life: **patience**, loyalty, **patience**, how much new couch cushions cost, **patience**, unconditional love, **patience**, how to unbolt a truck seat, **patience**, how to react to people who say, "Your dog did what?!", **patience**, laughter, I forgot...did I mention **patience**?

But the one thing that stands out most in my own mind was his overwhelming desire to see the face of the master. It seemed to be the supreme passion in his life (although I want to emphasize here that there is nothing special about my face; my wife's, Yes! But mine, no. In fact they could have used a picture of my face for those "Mr. Yeachy" stickers that are used to scare kids away from opening or drinking something poisonous). For some reason T-Bone had to frequently see the face of his master. When he did, he was fine; when he didn't, his separation anxiety kicked in. During the last few years of his life, even though he was almost completely blind, every so often at night he would get up and stick his face real close to either Kay's face or my face just to see if we were still there. He saw us (or probably rather smelled us) and then plopped back down to sleep. He always was a dog that wanted to sleep, sit, lie, and walk as close as possible to either Kay or I.

Maybe you've heard the phrase: "God is My Copilot." Maybe you've also heard the variation on that phrase: "Dog is My Copilot." In a way T-Bone taught Kay and I some things about God and His love for people.

Did you know that mankind suffers from its own form of "separation anxiety?" In a nutshell, the Bible says that God created Adam and Eve for a special purpose – that He might have a genuine love and deep friendship with them and that they (and all the "Adams" and "Eves" down through history to follow) might in turn have an authentic relationship with God. In fact, their hearts were created in such a way that if that bond was somehow broken they would experience their own form of "separation anxiety." In Genesis chapter three the Bible implies that on a daily basis God would sort of take time out from running the universe just to spend some time with Adam & Eve. He simply enjoyed going for strolls through the Garden of Eden with them. He couldn't wait to be with them! In fact if you looked at God's monthly planner, one slot of time every single day simply said, "Special Time with A&E!" The lives of Adam and Eve found fulfillment and satisfaction not in their job of taking care of the Garden nor in all of the "stuff" they had (and boy, did they have stuff!), but in their relationship with their heavenly Master. He walked with them and He talked with them. He got to look into their eyes (you know you can't really have a deep relationship with someone if you don't look into their eyes) and they got to see His face. Daily He saw their faces and they saw His face – and so they enjoyed complete rest and peace and there wasn't a trace of anxiety anywhere in their lives.

But something tragic occurred – Adam and Eve "sinned" and immediately that special relationship was broken. When God came to visit on that certain day in Genesis 3, instead of Adam and Eve running to God, for the very first time in their history they found themselves **running away from God!** That unique bond was shattered and God's heart was broken (it may have been the first day that the heavenly Master cried). The result? For the first time Adam and Eve experienced the full and catastrophic impact of "separation anxiety." As T-Bone's life was at times filled with misery and panic, so Adam and Eve became enveloped in misery, stress, chaos and emptiness – something was terribly wrong, desperately wrong, but they were totally incapable of knowing what to do or how to bring about a cure.

A Heatwarming Story of Life with One Really Nervous Dog

Throughout history men and women have tried on their own to heal that inner ache of the human heart, that inner separation anxiety, that inner "I know something is wrong or missing but I don't know what it is." People have tried money and riches, sex and drugs, jobs and hobbies, houses and stuff – all in a vain attempt to quiet that inner emptiness, that inner heartache, their own form of "separation anxiety." And just like with T-Bone, the behavior at times becomes destructive – they abuse drugs, they abuse people, they abuse food, they abuse themselves, they abuse just about anything there is to abuse. Like T-Bone, they try to escape (their problems), they pace (from worry and fretfulness), and they wear that "anxious smile mask" (on the outside they are smiling as though everything is fine, but inside they are crying and alone). They may be wearing prison stripes in solitary confinement in the most secure prison in our land or they may be wearing pinstripes and running one of the nation's Fortune 500 companies with an office suite the size of most homes, and yet there is an inner "something" that gnaws away at them daily and they can't find a cure.

But there is a cure, there is an answer! Even though Adam and Eve had sinned and run away from Him (and today's Adams and Eves are still doing the very same thing), the Father heart of God took the initiative to repair that relationship. They may have run away – **but He decided to run to them!** Some people may say that we showed extraordinary patience with T-Bone and his problems, but it is nothing compared to the patience that the Heavenly Master has shown toward the humanity that He desperately loves and longs to be with, and that He sent His Son Jesus to die for. There is a well-known verse in the Gospel of John (chapter three and verse sixteen) that states God's attitude toward those suffering from their own form of separation anxiety: "For God so loved the world that He Gave His only Son, that whosoever believes in Him should not perish but have everlasting life."

The ache, the cry, the crushing anxiety of the human heart can only be healed, so to speak, "by seeing the face of the Master" – by having a personal relationship with Jesus Christ. Whether you call it "getting saved," or "being born again" (Billy Graham's favorite term) or "getting religion," only Jesus Christ can fill that void and that cross-shaped vacuum in the human heart.

> The note from our vet was a real blessing to us, "To the Vander Ark's -- Please accept my most sincere condolences for the loss of T-Bone. Your devotion to him through all of his issues through the years was unparalleled. Take solace in the thought that he is in a good place now.

And perhaps you know all of this or you have heard it a thousand times before, but your picture of God is one of a harsh and stern Judge Who is ready, willing and eager to punish you.

But the picture that the Bible gives us is completely different from that. Remember the story of me walking T-Bone along old highway 61 and losing sight of him? What was my response? Was it, "Well dog, you didn't stay beside me (you "sinned"), so tough luck, you got yourself into this mess, you can get yourself out; so stay lost! You're on your own!" **NO!** When I realized he wasn't there, and that he couldn't see and couldn't hear and could easily get even more lost, I ran as fast as I could back up the trail to get to him before he wandered off into total lostness! **I RAN TO HIM! AS FAST AS I COULD!** And the Bible (in Luke chapter 15 – the "Prodigal Son" chapter) portrays God as a father with a broken heart longing for his rebellious and lost son to come home. And when the aged father catches sight of his long lost son, he does something rather amazing – he **runs to him with every ounce of strength he can muster!** And when they meet he embraces his bedraggled son and smothers him with love. **God is a running God! And God is running to you!!!** You may have run away a thousand times, you may feel that your anxiety could never be healed – but God is still running to you and has a cure for you!!!

Are you suffering from "separation anxiety?" The dictionary gives the definition of anxiety as, "A state of uncertainty and fear resulting from the anticipation of a threatening event (T-Bone's threatening event? Not being able to see the face of the master), often harming us physically and psychologically." Is there any anxiety deep inside of you that you can't figure out how to heal or how to cure? Give your heart to Jesus Christ today and let Him fill that void and ache in your heart. **He desperately loves you and knows your personal struggles!** Trying to cure separation anxiety in T-Bone proved to be very, very difficult. But curing separation anxiety in your heart is as simple as making this your sincere heart's prayer, "Heavenly Father, sometimes I feel just as miserable as how T-Bone must have felt, but I bring this inner ache and emptiness in my heart to You. I simply don't know how to cure this "separation anxiety" in my heart. I've tried, but I've failed. But I long to see Your Face – I long to have a personal relationship with You. And I want to see Your face as much as T-Bone wanted to see the face of his master the last few seconds of his life. I thank You that You loved me so much that You are running to me in my lostness -- that You sent Your Son to die for me on Calvary for all of the things that I have done wrong, for all of my sins. Jesus, I ask You to come into my heart today, forgive me of my sins and cure me of my own "separation anxiety." In Jesus Name I pray, Amen."

A Heatwarming Story of Life with One Really Nervous Dog

You will *never ever* be disappointed when you look into the Face of the Master!

Ps 42:1-2
As the deer panteth for the water brooks,
so panteth my soul for thee, O God.
My soul thirsteth for God, for the living God: when shall I come and see the face of God?

We Miss You 'Bone...

"A good dog never dies, he always stays, he walks beside you on crisp autumn days when frost is on the fields and winters drawing near, his head is within our hand in his old way."
-- Mary Carolyn Davies

April 15, 1993 – May 18th, 2006

A Heatwarming Story of Life with One Really Nervous Dog

"For God so loved the world, that He gave His only begotten Son, that whosoever believeth in Him should not perish, but have everlasting life."
John 3:16

About the author…

Dan and his wife Kay live in Duluth, Minnesota and have been married for 33 years. They have two daughters, two grandchildren, and two wonderful son-in-laws. Dan works as a database coordinator in the purchasing department of a local hospital/clinic facility. Kay has been working for local banks for the past 16 years, and as a result, Dan writes the stories and Kay writes the checks. They both love dogs, enjoy going to antique shops, flea markets, salvage yards, and just plain being together.

Quotes and Facts Sources

Page 7
"To his dog, every man is Napoleon; hence the constant popularity of dogs."
Aldous Huxley
"Dog Jokes and Quotes" on
www.publicityhound.com/dogjokebook

Page 10
"Outside of a dog, a book is man's best friend. Inside of a dog, it's too dark to read."
Groucho Marx
"Dog Jokes and Quotes" on
www.publicityhound.com/dogjokebook

Page 10
The oldest living dog in the world is either 27 (one claim) or 29 (another claim)
www.petsweekly.com & www.usatoday.com

Page 11
"We can judge the heart of a man by his treatment of animals."
Immanuel Kant
www.brainyquote.com:

Page 11
"Money will buy you a pretty good dog, but it won't buy the wag of his tail."
Anonymous
"Dog Jokes and Quotes" on
www.publicityhound.com/dogjokebook

Page 15
"Every boy should have two things: a dog, and a mother willing to let him have one." Anonymous
www.dogquotations.com

A Heatwarming Story of Life with One Really Nervous Dog

Page 15
"To err is human, to forgive canine."
Anonymous
www.dogtrainingcorner.com

Page 16
The Basenji is the only barkless dog in the world.
The oldest breed of dog native to North America is the Chihuahua.
www.petsweekly.com

Page 19
"A dog teaches a boy fidelity, perseverance, and to turn around three times before lying down"
Robert Benchley
"Dog Jokes and Quotes" on
www.publicityhound.com/dogjokebook

Page 19
"You can say any foolish thing to a dog, and the dog will give you a look that says, "My God, you're right! I never would've thought of that!"
Dave Barry
"Dog Jokes and Quotes" on
www.publicityhound.com/dogjokebook

Page 20
The Poodle haircut was originally meant to improve the dog's swimming abilities as a retriever, with the pom-poms left in place to warm their joints.
www.petsweekly.com

Page 26
"Things that upset a terrier may pass virtually unnoticed by a Great Dane."
-- Smiley Blanton
"Dog Jokes and Quotes" on
www.publicityhound.com/dogjokebook

Page 27
"No animal should ever jump up on the dining-room furniture unless absolutely certain that he can hold his own in the conversation."
Fran Lebowitz
"Dog Jokes and Quotes" on
www.publicityhound.com/dogjokebook

Page 27
"We've begun to long for the pitter-patter of little feet – so we bought a dog. Well, it's cheaper, and you get more feet."
Rita Rudner
"Dog Jokes and Quotes" on
www.publicityhound.com/dogjokebook

Page 28
There are 42 teeth in a dog's mouth.
In Paulding, Ohio, a policeperson is allowed to bite a dog in order to quiet him
From www.petsweekly.com

Page 36
6/100ths of a second! That's all it takes for dogs to locate the source of a sound. They can apparently swivel their ears like radar dishes.
www.petsweekly.com

Page 37
"I wonder if other dogs think poodles are members of a weird religious cult."
Rita Rudner
"Dog Jokes and Quotes" on
www.publicityhound.com/dogjokebook

Page 37
"The average dog is a nicer person than the average person."
Andy Rooney
"Dog Jokes and Quotes" on
www.publicityhound.com/dogjokebook

A Heatwarming Story of Life with One Really Nervous Dog

Page 38
"Did you ever walk into a room and forget why you walked in? I think that's how dogs spend their lives."
Sue Murphy
"Dog Jokes and Quotes" on
www.publicityhound.com/dogjokebook

page 44
"Don't accept your dog's admiration as conclusive evidence that you are wonderful."
Ann Landers
"Dog Jokes and Quotes" on
www.publicityhound.com/dogjokebook

Page 45
"Dogs feel very strongly that they should always go with you in the car, in case the need should arise for them to bark violently at nothing right in your ear."
Dave Barry
"Dog Jokes and Quotes" on
www.publicityhound.com/dogjokebook

Page 46
A 3-year-old Great Dane in California is apparently the world's tallest dog – he is 7 feet tall when upright.
www.local6.com

Page 53.
Dogs in Pennsylvania seeking to congregate in groups of three or more on private property must first have a permit signed by the mayor.
www.petsweekly.com

Page 54
A woman in Europe is claiming to be the owner of the world's smallest dog. The dog is four inches tall at the shoulder.
He is four inches from nose to tail and weighs just over a pound.
www.local6.com

Page 55
"I've seen a look in dogs' eyes, a quickly vanishing look of amazed contempt, and I am convinced that basically dogs think humans are nuts."
John Steinbeck
"Dog Jokes and Quotes" on
www.publicityhound.com/dogjokebook

Page 55
"In dog years, I'm dead"
Anonymous
"Dog Jokes and Quotes" on
www.publicityhound.com/dogjokebook

Page 56
"My dog is worried about the economy because Alpo is up to 99 cents a can. That's almost $7.00 in dog money."
Joe Weinstein
"Dog Jokes and Quotes" on
www.publicityhound.com/dogjokebook

Page 63
"I have sometimes thought of the final cause of dogs having such short lives and I am quite satisfied it is in compassion to the human race; for if we suffer so much in losing a dog after an acquaintance of ten to twelve years, what would it be if they were to double?"
Sir Walter Scott
www.dogquotations.com

Page 64
"The Dog was created especially for children. He is the god of frolic."
Henry Ward Beecher
www.quotationspage.com

A Heatwarming Story of Life with One Really Nervous Dog

Page 64
"Man himself cannot express love and humility by external signs so plainly as does a dog, when with dropping ears, hanging lips…and wagging tail, he meets his beloved master."
Charles Darwin
www.dogquotations.com

Page 64
"All knowledge, the totality of all questions and answers, is contained in the dog."
Franz Kafka
www.pawsitive.org

Page 65
"He is your friend, your partner, your defender, your dog. You are his life, his love, his leader. He will be yours, faithful and true, to the last beat of his heart. You owe it to him to be worthy of such devotion."
Anonymous
"Dog Jokes and Quotes" on
www.publicityhound.com/dogjokebook

Page 65
"A dog is the only thing on earth that loves you more than he loves himself."
Josh Billings
"Dog Jokes and Quotes" on
www.publicityhound.com/dogjokebook

Page 66
If a dog's prayers were answered, bones would rain from the sky."
Old Proverb
www.aboutdogsonline.com

Page 69
"Qui me amat, amet et canem meum."
(Who loves me will love my dog also)
St. Bernard
www.deafdogs.org

Page 70
"There is honor in being a dog." Aristotle
www.ameridogs.com

Page 71
"Dear Master," I explained to Saint Peter, "I'd rather stay here, outside the pearly gates. I won't be a nuisance, I won't even bark, I'll be very patient and wait. I'll be here, chewing on a celestial bone no matter how long you may be. I'd miss you so much if I went in alone. It wouldn't be heaven for me.
Unknown
www.angeldoggie.com

Page 71
"If I have any beliefs about immortality, it is that certain dogs I have known will go to heaven, and very, very few persons."
James Thurber
"Dog Jokes and Quotes" on
www.publicityhound.com/dogjokebook

Page 72
"In the beginning, God created man, but seeing him so feeble, He gave him the dog."
Toussenel
www.dribbleglass.com

Page 73
"…no mere man has ever seen, heard, or even imagined what wonderful things God has ready for those who love the Lord."
Ken Taylor
The Living Bible

Page 80
"I have sometimes thought of the final cause of dogs having such short lives and I am quite satisfied it is in compassion to the human race; for if we suffer so much in losing a dog after an acquaintance of ten to twelve years, what would it be if they were to double?"
Sir Walter Scott
www.dogquotations.com

A Heatwarming Story of Life with One Really Nervous Dog

Page 81
"Heaven goes by favour. If it went by merit, you would stay out and your dog would go in."
Mark Twain
www.sagekeep.com/dogquotes

Page 81
"I care not for a man's religion whose dog and cat are not the better for it."
Abraham Lincoln
www.dogquotes.com

Page 82
Near this spot are deposited the remains of one who possessed beauty without vanity, strength without insolence, courage without ferocity, and all the virtues of man without his vices. This praise, which would be unmeaning flattery if inscribed over human ashes, is but a just tribute to the memory of "Boatswain" a dog, who was born at Newfoundland, May 1803 and died at Newstead Abbey, November 18, 1808.
John Cam Hobhouse/Lord Byron
www.wikipedia.org

Page 94
"A good dog never dies, he always stays, he walks beside you on crisp autumn days when frost is on the fields and winters drawing near, his head is within our hand in his old way."
Mary Carolyn Davies
www.angeldoggie.com